What in the World Is a Flute?

Mary Elizabeth Salzmann

Consulting Editor, Diane Craig, M.A./Reading Specialist

A Division of ABDO

ABDO
Publishing Company

visit us at www.abdopublishing.com

Published by ABDO Publishing Company, a division of ABDO, P.O. Box 398166, Minneapolis, Minnesota 55439. Copyright © 2012 by Abdo Consulting Group, Inc. International copyrights reserved in all countries. No part of this book may be reproduced in any form without written permission from the publisher. Super SandCastle™ is a trademark and logo of ABDO Publishing Company.

Printed in the United States of America, North Mankato, Minnesota
092011
012012

 PRINTED ON RECYCLED PAPER

Editor: Elissa Mann
Content Developer: Nancy Tuminelly
Cover and Interior Design: Colleen Dolphin, Mighty Media, Inc.
Photo Credits: iStockphoto (Anna Malanushenko), Shutterstock, Thinkstock

Library of Congress Cataloging-in-Publication Data

Salzmann, Mary Elizabeth, 1968-

What in the world is a flute? / Mary Elizabeth Salzmann.

p. cm. -- (Musical instruments)

ISBN 978-1-61783-205-5

1. Flute--Juvenile literature. I. Title.

ML935S25 2012   7720

788.3'219--dc23

2011023170

Super SandCastle™ books are created by a team of professional educators, reading specialists, and content developers around five essential components— phonemic awareness, phonics, vocabulary, text comprehension, and fluency—to assist young readers as they develop reading skills and strategies and increase their general knowledge. All books are written, reviewed, and leveled for guided reading, early reading intervention, and Accelerated Reader® programs for use in shared, guided, and independent reading and writing activities to support a balanced approach to literacy instruction.

Contents

What Is a

A flute is a musical instrument.

Flute?

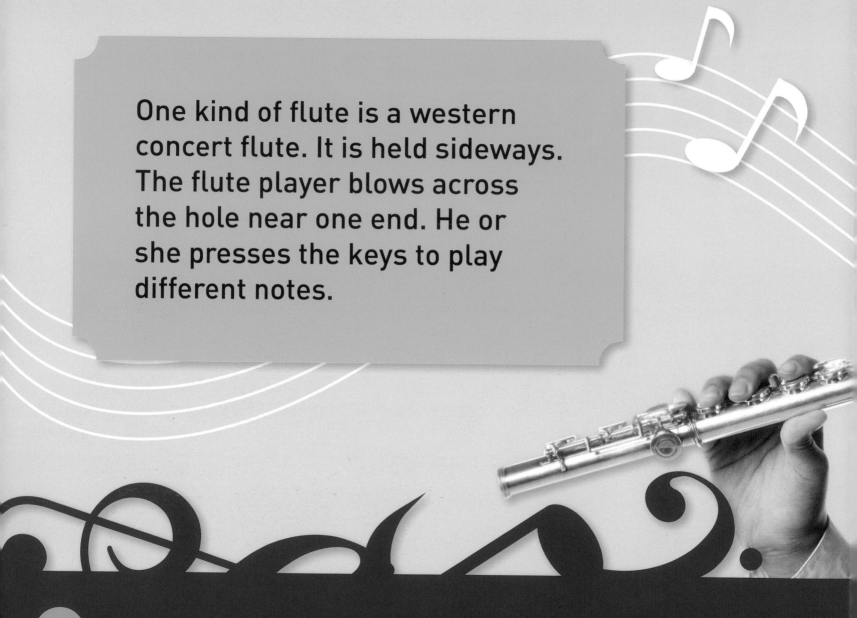

One kind of flute is a western concert flute. It is held sideways. The flute player blows across the hole near one end. He or she presses the keys to play different notes.

A recorder is a kind of flute.
It can be made of wood or **plastic**.
A recorder has holes on its side.
The recorder player blows into
the end of the recorder. He or she
covers some of the holes to play
different notes.

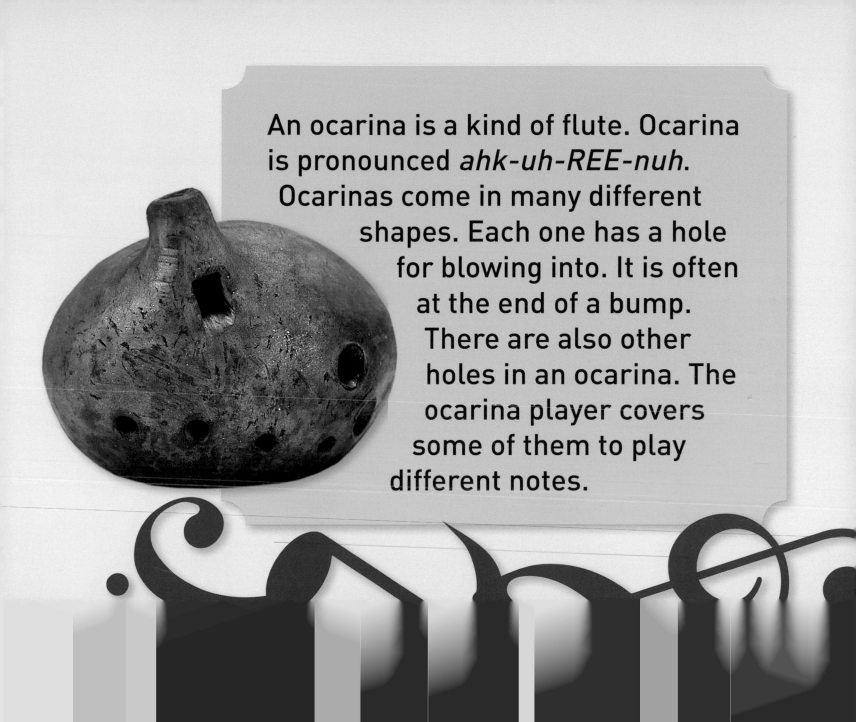

An ocarina is a kind of flute. Ocarina is pronounced *ahk-uh-REE-nuh*. Ocarinas come in many different shapes. Each one has a hole for blowing into. It is often at the end of a bump. There are also other holes in an ocarina. The ocarina player covers some of them to play different notes.

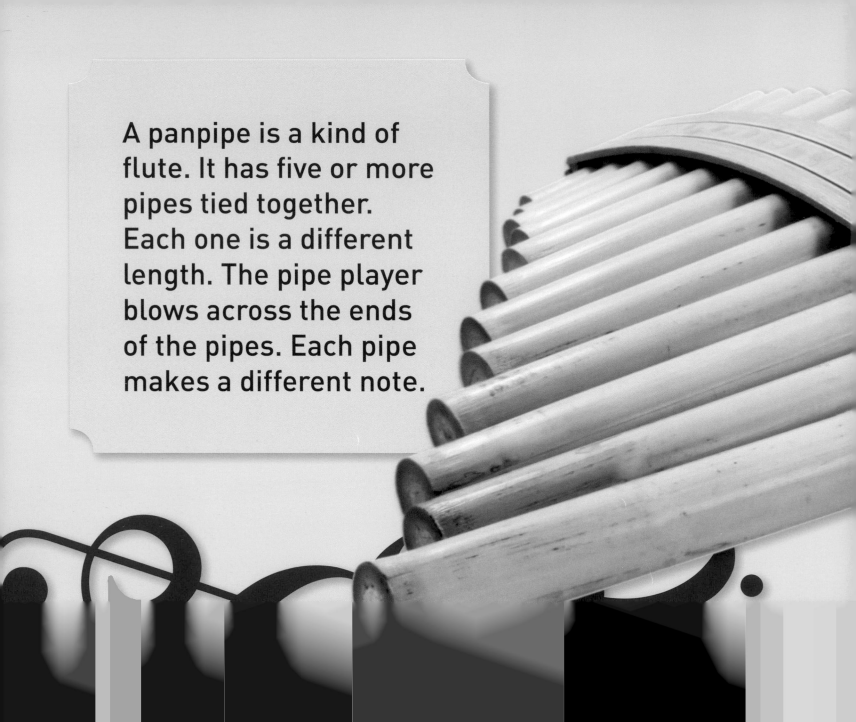

A panpipe is a kind of flute. It has five or more pipes tied together. Each one is a different length. The pipe player blows across the ends of the pipes. Each pipe makes a different note.

Let's Play

the Flute!

Sarah practices a song on the concert flute. The **sheet music** tells her which notes to play.

Ryan is playing an ocarina.
He learned how to play
from his grandfather.

Jan has a recorder **lesson** every Friday. She and her teacher play a song together.

19

Tim is playing a panpipe.
His panpipe has 11 pipes.

Find the Flute

a.

b.

c.

d.

22

a. piano

b. flute (correct)

c. clarinet

d. violin

Flute Quiz

1. Western concert flutes are held sideways. True or False?

2. A recorder has holes on its side. True or False?

3. Ocarinas come in many shapes. True or False?

4. Sarah practices a song on the recorder. True or False?

5. Tim's panpipe has ten pipes. True or False?

ANSWERS: 1. true 2. true 3. true 4. false 5. false

Glossary

lesson – a period of time when a skill or topic is studied or taught.

plastic – a man-made material that is light and strong and can be made into different shapes.

sheet music – a sheet of paper with the notes to a song printed on it.